Let's Roll

STOCK CARS

by Candice Ransom

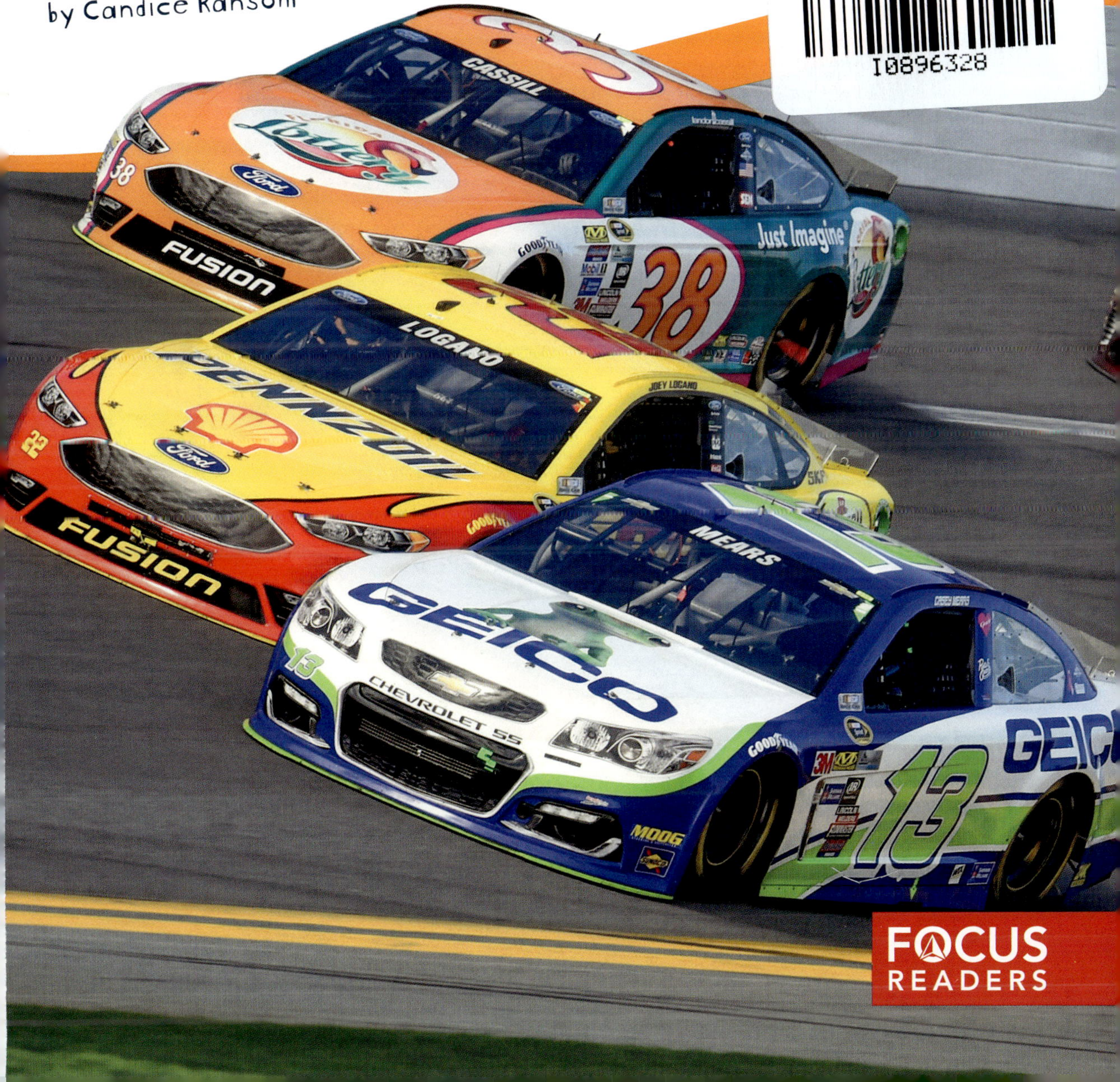

FOCUS READERS

North Star
EDITIONS

www.northstareditions.com

Produced for North Star Editions by Red Line Editorial.

Photographs ©: Nigel Kinrade/NKP/AP Images, cover, 1; Action Sports Photography/Shutterstock Images, 4–5, 9, 14, 18, 22–23, 25, 29; Wilfredo Lee/AP Images, 7; Ann Rosener/FSA/OWI Collection/Library of Congress, 10–11; AP Images, 12; Daniel Huerlimann-Beelde/Shutterstock Images, 16–17, 21, 26–27

ISBN
978-1-63517-052-8 (hardcover)
978-1-63517-108-2 (paperback)
978-1-63517-209-6 (ebook pdf)
978-1-63517-159-4 (hosted ebook)

Library of Congress Control Number: 2016951028

Printed in the United States of America
Mankato, MN
August, 2017

About the Author

Candice Ransom used to ride on her stepfather's tractor. She loved trips in their green pickup, and she thinks old cars are the best. When she isn't writing books for children, she is driving on the back roads of Virginia in her own little red truck.

TABLE OF CONTENTS

20
KENSETH
DOLLAR GENERAL
11
HAMLIN
FedEx Express
CAMRY
4
HARVICK
FREAKY FAST
78
TRUEX JR.
Bass Pro Shops
TRACKER
FUSION
KYLE BUSCH
m&m's

CHAPTER 1

MAKING HISTORY

It's race day in Daytona Beach, Florida. The Daytona 500 always opens the NASCAR racing season. On this day, February 21, 2016, stock cars whirl around the track. The drivers are on the last lap.

Denny Hamlin (11) cuts inside as Matt Kenseth (20) loses the lead in the 2016 Daytona 500.

They have driven nearly 500 miles (807 km).

Matt Kenseth speeds around the first turn. He is in the lead, with Martin Truex Jr. behind him. Denny Hamlin is in fourth place.

On the final turn, Hamlin passes the third-place car. Then he pulls

FUN FACT

The first Daytona 500 was in 1958. Lee Petty won by only 2 feet (0.6 m).

Hamlin (11) crosses the finish line a split second ahead of Truex (78) to win the Daytona 500.

even with Truex. Hamlin darts left, and Kenseth falls behind.

Hamlin and Truex race side-by-side over the finish line. Hamlin wins by inches! It's the closest finish in the history of the Daytona 500. Hamlin gets out of his car and raises his fists in the air. He and his pit crew are ready to celebrate.

FUN FACT

Denny Hamlin beat Martin Truex by 0.001 seconds. That's three times faster than the blink of an eye.

Denny Hamlin celebrates his thrilling Daytona 500 victory.

AB

DIRT ROADS, FAST CARS

In the 1930s and 1940s, people raced one another in their own cars. The cars were called stock cars because they were bought from auto dealers. The races were usually held on dirt roads.

In the early days of stock car racing, some people modified their engines to make their cars go faster.

Stock cars race at Daytona Beach in the 1950s.

People showed up to watch cars tear up these dirt tracks. Stock car racing was born.

Drivers started to modify their cars. These changes made the cars go faster. Promoters sold tickets to the races. They offered cash prizes to the winners.

FUN FACT

In 1948, the first NASCAR race was held in Daytona Beach, Florida. The track was on both the road and the beach.

Richard Petty, who won the Daytona 500 seven times, is one of the greatest stock car drivers of all time.

Driver and promoter Bill France believed stock car racing should be an organized sport. In 1947, he created the National Association for Stock Car Auto Racing (NASCAR).

Under NASCAR rules, races would have regular schedules. At the end of the racing season, one driver would be crowned national champion.

CLASSES OF STOCK CARS

In the 1940s, there were two classes of stock cars. "Modified" cars were altered to go faster. Drivers added more powerful engines, removed lights and mufflers, and strapped the doors shut. "Strictly stock" cars were passenger vehicles taken straight from auto showrooms.

Nation
MONSTER
54
CAM

BUILT FOR SPEED

Stock cars start with a steel-tube frame. The **roll cage** protects the driver. The car's body is made of thin steel sheets. The smooth tires are called racing slicks.

Stock cars go through several sets of tires during each race.

Stock car drivers wear helmets and fire suits to stay as safe as possible.

These tires grip the track better than regular tires, especially on turns.

The driver climbs into the car through a net-covered window. The cockpit contains the ignition switch, the steering wheel, and a radio button for talking to the crew.

FUN FACT

Drivers use spotters who tell them when to pass. Spotters use radios to communicate with their drivers.

The cockpit also has a rearview mirror and a gearshift. The **tachometer** measures the engine's power.

How do stock cars go so fast? They use eight-**cylinder** engines.

COLORFUL CARS

Most stock cars are wrapped in vinyl sheets. Designs are created on a computer. A special printer produces sticky sheets that behave like giant bumper stickers. Two or three people wrap the car. They use blowtorches to smooth out air bubbles.

PARTS OF A STOCK CAR

A regular car on the street uses approximately 200 **horsepower**. NASCAR engines are much more powerful. They zoom to 750 horsepower.

pepsi
pepsi
Con-way
Con-way
Con-way
16
Ford
GOODYEAR
MAC TOOLS
Dupli-Color
FREIG
Solutions
WALLACE
TOYOTA
WIX
GOODYEAR
MSD

CHAPTER 4

SAFER, FASTER STOCK CARS

Stock cars sometimes crash. But new materials help make the cars safer. Hoods and trunk lids are made of **carbon fiber**. The windows are made of a plastic that does not shatter.

Thanks to new technology, crashes are less dangerous today than they were in the past.

Technology also helps stock cars go faster. When a car moves, it pushes against the air. A splitter under the front bumper splits the air. Some air goes under the car,

FULL OF AIR

Stock cars are tested in a wind tunnel with 22 fans that are 18 feet (5.5 m) tall. Wind speeds can reach hurricane strength. Computers record pressures in the floor beneath the car. A stream of smoke shows the path of air traveling over the car. Racing teams analyze the reports. They can make adjustments so their cars will be even faster.

Downforce helps cars stay on the track during turns.

and some flows over the hood. The **spoiler** on the trunk lid lets air stream around the car. This airflow creates **downforce** that presses the car down to the ground.

HOW IT WORKS

USING AIR TO GO FASTER

Stock car drivers use the science of airflow to win races. A common technique is called **drafting**. The lead car punches a "hole" in the air. The second car follows so close that it is almost touching. Air flows up and over the lead car's roof and continues over the second car. The second car is pulled along.

If the second car bumps the lead car, the lead car goes faster. The second car goes faster, too, because the pulling air is stronger.

Drafting cars travel faster than one car alone.

LAS VEGAS MOTOR SPEEDWAY

FOCUS ON

STOCK CARS

Write your answers on a separate piece of paper.

1. Write a sentence that summarizes the main idea of Chapter 3.
2. Do you think stock cars have enough safety equipment? Why or why not?
3. Who won the 2016 Daytona 500?
   - A. Martin Truex Jr.
   - B. Matt Kenseth
   - C. Denny Hamlin
4. Why don't stock cars have windshields made of glass?
   - A. Glass would not be as safe as plastic.
   - B. Glass would be too heavy.
   - C. Glass would be too expensive.

5. What does **modify** mean in this book?

   A. to drive faster

   B. to make changes

   C. to spend money

Drivers started to **modify** their cars. These changes made the cars go faster.

6. What does **promoters** mean in this book?

   A. people who organize events

   B. people who buy tickets

   C. people who win races

Promoters sold tickets to the races. They offered cash prizes to the winners.

Answer key on page 32.

GLOSSARY

carbon fiber
A strong, lightweight material made of carbon.

cylinder
The chamber where gasoline is burned and turned into power.

downforce
A force produced by air resistance that pushes down on a vehicle.

drafting
The practice of cars following one another very closely to travel faster.

horsepower
A unit for measuring an engine's power.

roll cage
A frame built inside a vehicle that protects the driver if the vehicle rolls onto its roof.

spoiler
A blade that helps regulate airflow.

tachometer
An instrument that measures the speed of an engine's rotation.

TO LEARN MORE

BOOKS

Challen, Paul. *NASCAR Racing*. New York: PowerKids Press, 2015.

Long, Dustin. *NASCAR Racing*. Minneapolis: Abdo Publishing, 2015.

Reinke, Beth Bence. *Behind the Wheel of a Stock Car*. Mankato, MN: The Child's World, 2016.

NOTE TO EDUCATORS

Visit **www.focusreaders.com** to find lesson plans, activities, links, and other resources related to this title.

INDEX

Answer Key: 1. Answers will vary; **2.** Answers will vary; **3.** C; **4.** A; **5.** B; **6.** A